more
Theme Hotels

Imprint

The Deutsche Bibliothek is registering
this publication in the Deutsche
Nationalbibliographie; detailed biblio-
graphical information can be found on
the internet at http://dnb.ddb.de

ISBN 978-3-03768-009-4

© 2009 by Braun Publishing AG
www.braun-publishing.ch

1st edition 2009

Project coordinator: Annika Schulz
Editorial staff: Dagmar Glück,
                        Nadja Mahler
Translation: Cosima Talhouni
Graphic design: Michaela Prinz

more
Theme Hotels

Frederik Prinz

BRAUN

Contents
more Theme Hotels

Foreword

more Theme Hotels

In the course of history, the increase in travel led to the development of temporary accommodations and services, which can be summed up under the main heading of 'board and lodging'. In Europe, these included the medieval hospices that were set up for travelers such as St. James pilgrims. In South America, the tampus along the Inca routes provided lodging and board for messengers, public officials and warriors, while also serving as material warehouses. Other examples of early 'professional' rental accommodations included the military fortified caravansaries located on key trade routes in the Persian cultural realm or the Japanese ryokan, which present a particularly striking example of a specific cultural context. The guests are provided with slippers with which they enter the mat-covered complex. In the rented room, food is served on a side table, and the sleeping area is provided by spreading a futon.

The term 'hotel' in its contemporary meaning dates back to the late 18th century. It was around this time that first establishments emerged across Europe, offering guests an equal degree of board and lodging services as 'all-round' services. The hotel sector experienced a particular boom between the 19th and 20th century as part of the overall construction boom of the industrialization era. During this Belle Epoque, members of the bourgeoisie gained in influence and focused their attention on a well-to-do to glamorous living environment. As a newly emerged elite, they also demanded travel accommodations in line with their high standards of living. This resulted in prestigious urban architecture and luxurious spa hotels in remote locations. Following World War II, renewed economic growth provided a broader basis for the hotel sector in industrialized nations. Hotel chains in particular created travel accommodations that were also accessible to a less wealthy group of persons. This, however, usually implied the standardization of offered services. In Japan, a new model of mass accommodation emerged with the capsule hotels, which provide guests with sleeping cells arranged in a honey-comb style.

The increasingly diverse lifestyles of modern individuals, coupled with simultaneously increasing mobility, also affected the hotel sector, which experienced a creative revival as opposed to the above-described tendencies. Therefore, the international hotel landscape is impressively diverse. How is this diversity expressed? In addition to the basic elements – reception, rooms and dining services – the range of services has expanded to meet individual requirements. In conjunction with architects and designers, hotel operators want to provide their establishments with a unique and distinguished profile to encourage their guests to come back. Unusual designs and exceptional room concepts create an unmistakable recognition value for each of the special buildings. Between the obligatory framework of check-in and check-out there is an almost unlimited range of design options and conceptual focuses. This book showcases this variety of concepts by paying tribute to the diversity of hotel architecture. Following the great success of the volume Theme Hotels, which presented the most outstanding European hotels, More Theme Hotels now presents hotels from around the globe in eight categories: Historical Ties, Mountain Pastime, Designed Spaces, Luxury Residences, Wellness Islands, Urban Hideouts and Countryside Hotels.

Historical insinuations are also found beyond the traditional European hotels, for example when the architecture and inventory reflect elements of Arab exclusivity or the style of the Japanese ryokan with its simple choice of materials and clearly laid out room structure. Other concepts included avant-garde constructions embedded in snow and mountain landscapes, which allow an athletic audience to delve into an almost surreal spa experience. Wellness oases are committed to the current social trend towards a healthy and at the same time pleasurable lifestyle, by catering to the desire for physical, spiritual and emotional well-being through a scope of services ranging from massages to stimulating light installations. The dichotomy of the city and countryside is a significant contrast of hotel architecture. The range of rural hotels extends from rather rustic inns with building materials based on nature up to large-windowed buildings that separate guests from the idyll of the beach by a mere few centimeters of glass. In contrast, city hotels often convey a feeling of security and a friendly to inspiring refuge beyond the hustle and bustle of the surrounding metropolis. Design hotels attempt to convey a feeling of individuality and an exclusive lifestyle for guests through the extravagant and unique design of every single room.

Thus hotel architecture offers an unlimited scope of experimentation in search for an unforgettable impression. Based on the spatial givens and the respective con-

cept, the buildings vary from high-rises to small rural inns and present highly intricate as well as very simple geometric shapes. Building materials such as ice, wood or concrete are used according to the desired effect and the regional availability. The respective interior designs range from ornamental to expressionist, and from ostentatious or simple.

Despite all their differences, hotels are distinguished by one common characteristic – they offer travelers a place to stay away from home based on their individual desires and transport them into a one-of-a-kind world in a professionally implemented dominant overall concept. Thus the formula 'board and lodging' has turned into the formula 'board and lodging+ X'. It is this significant addition of "X", which turns modern hotel design into a never ceasing source of inspiration for observers who are fond of architecture.

Frederik Prinz

historical

Puro Hotel
Hotel Mals
Hegia
Opus Hotel
New
Gihzan Orts
Riva Lofts

ties

Kokenhof
al del Rey
Palace
ont des Ôtes
Hotel Ritter
estic Hotel
en Fulva
Ace Hotel

Architects:
JOI-Design
Innenarchitekten
GmbH
Client:
Kind Hörgeräte
Betriebs GmbH
Completion:
2006

above:
Exterior view
below:
Interior view
right:
Reception detail

Großburg-wedel

Kokenhof

The historical building from the year 1556 was already loaded in a huge container

waiting to be shipped to the USA, where it was supposed to be used as a restaurant, showcasing typical German 'Gemütlichkeit'. Yet this was not meant to be and 20 years ago the building found a new home in the vicinity of Hanover, where it was utilized as a hotel. In 2005, the architects transformed this old timbered house into a boutique hotel. Balancing history and modernity they turned the room structure upside down. The result is a linear and expanded clear, contemporary room topology. The original wooden beams and clay brick stonework are now combined with illuminated glass surfaces and unruffled white walls. The design is reduced to calm powerful surfaces, representing modernity as well as history with glass and bog oak. The colors are limited – with horizontal stone surfaces creating accents in discrete shades of cream. The open room structure repeatedly presents astonishing new aspects.

above:
Reception
mid:
Conference room
above right:
Conference room

below:
Restaurant
below right:
Floor plan

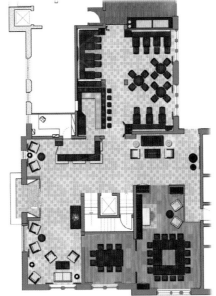

Architect:
Álvaro Planchuelo
Designers:
Álvaro Planchuelo,
K & E Brabandt
Client:
South Point's Hotel SA
Completion:
2006

above:
Reception
below:
Patio
right:
Reception

14

Palma de Mallorca

Puro Hotel

This city hotel resulted from the restoration of a residential building in the neighborhood of La Lonja, the former port of Palma de Mallorca, one of the principal areas of medieval trade in the western Mediterranean. The concept was based on the theme of 'the art of travelling' or 'knowing how to travel'. The team of architects and interior decorators interpreted this by trying to harmoniously bring together the essential traits of some of the big cultures in history. The Mediterranean sensual flair is represented by the proper building, while Oriental serenity is present in the wall decorations, roofs and materials of the areas and rooms. The materials of the decorative objects and furniture are clearly accentuated by the magic and exoticism of the Arab-Hindu culture. Light, water, fire and the landscape are constantly present.

above:
Opio restaurant
below:
First floor plan

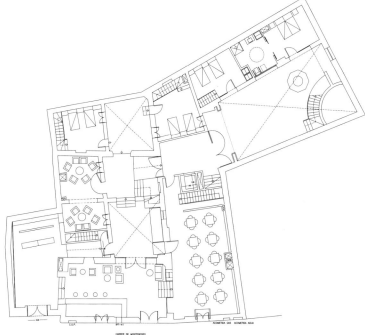

above:
Bathroom
below:
Room Puro Joy

Architect:
Javier Betancourt
Designer:
Kuky Mora-Figueroa
Client:
Benchamark Capital
S.L.
Completion:
2007

above:
Restaurant
below:
Patio
right:
Entrance

18

Seville

Corral del Rey

Amalgamating Mudejar designs, the 17th century Casa Palacio, Corral del Rey, situ-
ated in the heart of Seville a few minutes away from the Cathedral, in the old quarter of Barrio Alfalfa, has been meticulously restored into a private luxury hotel. Striking a fine balance between historic charm and modern design, the architectural features include original Roman marble columns, wrought-iron balcony railings, terracotta tiles, and wooden carved beams. A blend of old and modern, inspired by sensitivity and imagination, the fine art work is accentuated by a subtle Lutron controlled lighting scheme. The well-appointed bedrooms, situated around a central patio, are decorated with classic Nicole Fabre fabrics. The combination with pale olive green cabinets and stylish oak paneled floors provides an understated modern touch.

above:
Meeting room
mid:
Junior suite

below:
Junior suite bathroom

above:
Deluxe room
mid:
Deluxe room

below:
Floor plans

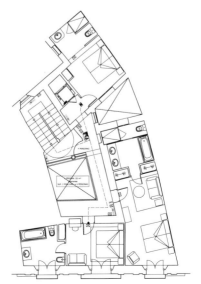
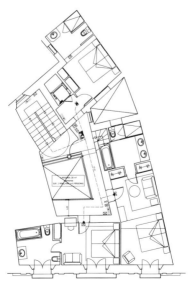

Architects:
Andromeda
International SRL
Designers:
Andromeda
International –
Richmond
International
Client:
Starwood Westin
Completion:
2008

above:
Fine dining restaurant
below:
Main gallery
right:
Main entrance

Versailles

Trianon Palace Hotel

royal residence with a splendid view of the Palace. It is not just a hotel, but a historic location... the Treaty of Versailles was actually signed in one of its rooms, the Clémenceau. Andromeda has created the hotel's decorative lighting, which combines with the setting of each room to enhance the architectural and functional context. The result is a mix of Murano handmade glass structures characterized by different styles and moods. The entrance and galleries feature for the first time the Knit element, designed by Karim Rashid, in a structural and decorative concept developed by Michela Vianello, Art Director of Andromeda. In the la Veranda brasserie five Le Roi c'est moi, the classical style is reinterpreted with a touch of contemporary.

above:
Dining-hall
below:
Chandelier in dining-hall

above:
Fine dining restaurant Pearl

below:
Detail Pearl

Architects:
Xavier Leibar –
Jean-Marie Seigneurin
Client:
Monsieur et Madame
Daguin
Completion:
2004

left:
Entrance
right:
Dining room

26

Hasparren
Maison d'hôtes Hegia

This project originated in a meeting in which the clients expressed their enthusiasm

and passion for implementing a very distinguished type of vision. Their request consisted of bringing an eighteenth century farm building in harmony with their 'art de recevoir'. The difficulty of this request caused the architects to work very cautiously, keeping in mind that the precondition for any design concept was to primarily pay attention to the site and the existing building. This process of gradual awakening and sensitive analysis was judiciously accompanied by the client's expressed desire for the concepts of comfort, pleasure and sharing. This led to the conception of five rooms designed like individual spaces, in which each element contributes to creating environments in which serenity is of the utmost priority.

above:
Bedroom
below:
Detail bedroom
right:
Bathroom

Architects:
JOI-Design
Innenarchitekten
GmbH
Client:
Dominic Müller
Completion:
2008

above:
Reception
below:
Lobby

Durbach

The Hotel Ritter (German for knight) has recently undergone a significant update.

Hotel Ritter

Breaking away from its previous outdated image, the hotel interior has managed to evolve from its humble beginnings, making a leap into the style-conscious age. White German cuckoo clocks from the black forest region welcome guests on a fuchsia colored wall, featuring the international time zones of New York, Rio, Tokyo and Durbach. In the lobby, modern furniture is mixed with old. Browns and cream tones dominate, but are broken up by a pink-colored floral sofa – reminiscent of something you'd expect to see in your grandmother's house. Throughout the lobby, the shades of cream are interspersed by multiple-colored cushions, which add color and a provide a link to the pink sofa. A knight in armor guards the way to the new lobby.

above:
View of bar and reception
mid:
Private room in restaurant
above right:
Suite

below:
Pool area of spa
below right:
Sketch of private rooms

Architects:
Dan S. Hanganu
Architects
Designer:
Yabu Pushelberg
Client:
John deC. Evans
Completion:
2007

above:
Exterior view
below:
Entrance hall with reception

34

Montreal

Opus Hotel Montreal is a unique boutique hotel that blends contemporary style

Opus Hotel

Opus Hotel Montreal is a unique boutique hotel that blends contemporary style and design with a nod to the historic with a chic Montreal touch. The original avant-garde structure, built in 1914 by Joseph-Arthur Godin, was the first poured concrete building in North America. Created in an Art Nouveau style, the building featured little ornamentation, save for a signature curving staircase. This simplicity of design is reflected in the unmistakably modern concrete addition, created by architect Dan Hanganu of Montreal and interior designer Yabu Pushelberg of New York, both winners of the prestigious 'Platinum Circle Award'. Inside, Opus Hotel Montreal's intimate one hundred and thirty-six guest-rooms combine sleek minimalism with luxurious comfort. Opus Hotel Montreal provides the service and amenities of a luxury hotel in a stylish and intimate environment.

above:
Foyer Godin
mid:
Restaurant

below:
Mezzanine

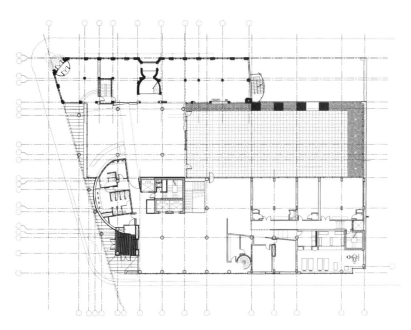

above:
Floor plan
below:
Detail Presidential suite

Architects:
Ministry of Design
Designer:
Colin Seah
Client:
Loh Lik Peng
Completion:
2006

above:
Restaurant
below:
Lobby

Singapore
New Majestic Hotel

The New Majestic Hotel comprises four adjoining three-floor commercial buildings, which have been combined and adapted for re-use as an exclusive 30-bedroom boutique hotel. The historical listed façades of the commercial buildings, which date back to 1927, were retained and restored. In a unique design concept, reflecting the inner struggle of a mistress, a curvilinear stairway expressing feminine sensuality was introduced into the hotel as its central feature. The stairway connects the rugged ground floor lobby (where the original ceilings have been retained showing the ravages of time) to the new swimming pool deck on the second floor, symbolizing her passage from initial shame to final relaxation. Terrazzo flooring, a formerly popular but now almost forgotten trade, is used in the front lobby to reinforce the theme of nostalgia.

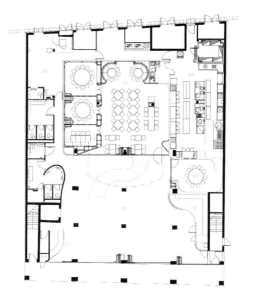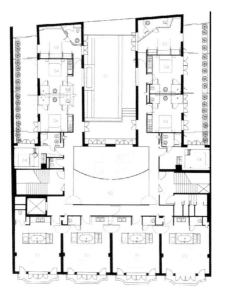

above:
1st and 2nd floor plan
mid:
The Aqua room
right:
Hanging bedroom

below:
View room

Architects:
Kengo Kuma &
Architects
Client:
Ginzan Onsen Fujiya
Completion:
2006

above:
Exterior view at night
below:
Front view

42

Obanazawa

Ginzan Onsen Fujiya

Architecturally, the project consisted of 'a large scale refurbishment' rather than

the construction of an entirely new building, which would have abandoned the idea of a 'three-story wooden house'. Instead, the existing structure was preserved by removing the concrete parts that had been added when the hotel was enlarged, and checking every single wooden part to replace the worn pieces with new wood to enhance the building's earthquake-resistance. The existing façade was renovated utilizing wood from the original 100-year old hotel while the interior space was reorganized by the insertion of an atrium. This atrium is surrounded by a delicate screen made of 4 mm-wide slits of bamboo (Sumushiko), while Dalle de Verre, an almost-transparent stained glass, is fit into the opening that faces the outside.

above:
Detail lobby
mid:
Interior view
above right:
Lobby

below:
Detail of façade
below right:
Cross section

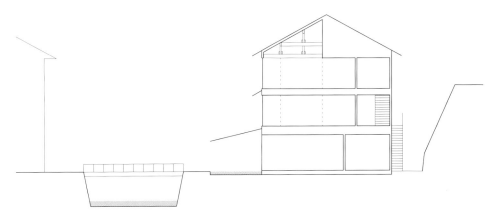

above left:
Interior room
above:
Interior

below:
Bathroom in open room
below left:
Wooden wall construction

Architects:
Ace Hotel Portland
Designers:
Atelier Ace
Client:
Ace Hotel Group
Completion:
2007

above:
Exterior view
below:
Front desk

Portland

Ace Hotel Portland is the result of the renovation of an old hotel built in 1912. Many

Ace Hotel

of its original details, such as the deep cast-iron roll-top baths and capacious sinks, have been retained and refurbished. As much of the historical character as possible was retained and combined with clean lines to create a look of warm minimalism. The team at the Ace also turned to local artists, suppliers and craftsmen for a mix of modern and vintage elements to create a distinctive Ace aesthetic which at the same time reflects the hotel's locality. One of the most important aims was that rooms should not look like hotel rooms – instead resembling private homes. Rather than a $15-a-drink cocktail bar, the hotel offers Portland's legendary Stumptown Coffee Roasters, the comfortable communal-seating Clyde Common restaurant, and the retro diner-themed Kenny and Zuke's Delicatessen.

above:
Hotel lobby

below:
Floor plan

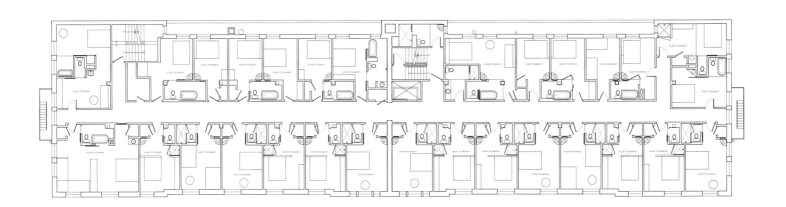

above:
Interior room
mid:
Hotel room

below:
Bath corner

Architect:
Claudio Nardi
Architetto
Client:
M.C. Details S.r.l.
Completion:
2007

above:
Meeting room
below:
Exterior view of garden pool area

Florence

This group of buildings was a small factory in 1880. Today the nine suites are decorated

Riva Lofts

in the style of French studios, blending a metropolitan lifestyle with a welcoming and domestic atmosphere. The interiors, all distinctly unique in size, shape and style, boast a well-defined and recognizable character. Fusion is the leading theme behind the structure's conception: pure and contemporary, the warm atmosphere in these distinctive spaces is due to a series of recovered historic elements – modern antiques, 1950's furniture, old and new materials, wood and Corian, and examples of sophisticated design. Riva Loft is made up of nine suites, all with independent entrances and well-equipped kitchens, which range from 30 to 100 square meters in size. In spite of its location close to the old city center of Florence, the Riva Lofts 'home for guests' is particularly quiet and peaceful thanks to its location in an area of parks and gardens.

above:
Living space of ground
floor suite
above right:
Loft studio

below:
Interior view of a
two level-suite
below right:
Floor plan

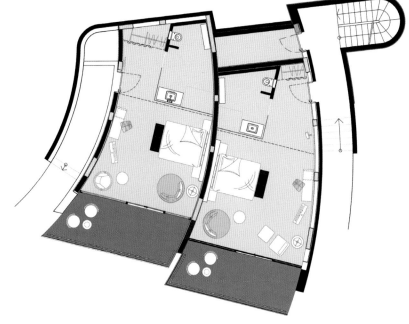

mountain

pastime

Architect:
Åke Larsson/
ICEHOTEL AB
Designers:
always different
Client:
ICEHOTEL AB
Completion:
2008

above:
Entrance
below:
Main hall

Jukkasjärvi

Just a few meters away from the Torne River, high above the Arctic Circle in Swedish

Icehotel

Lapland, the Icehotel is as close to its source as possible in terms of building materials. The giant, two-ton blocks of ice that are used to make the walls, pillars, furniture and sculptures are harvested annually from the slow-moving Torne river. The massive ice blocks are then stored in climate-controlled, subzero warehouses through the summer and autumn months until winter's pristine white landscape and teeth-chattering temperatures announce the start of another Icehotel season. Once construction is under way, water is pumped up from the Torne river and fed into huge snow cannons, which then spray the snow that will be used to build the basic structure of the hotel. This moist snow is then collected and sprayed on top of huge steel forms — a casting process which, after the snow is allowed to freeze and the forms are removed, will reveal the walls and vaulted ceilings of the Icehotel.

left:
Crystal ice church
above:
Room Contact

below:
Detail Absolut Icebar
Jukkasjärvi

above:
Room 22:05
mid:
Room Meander
above right:
The Forest Suite

below:
Reception
below right:
Floor plan

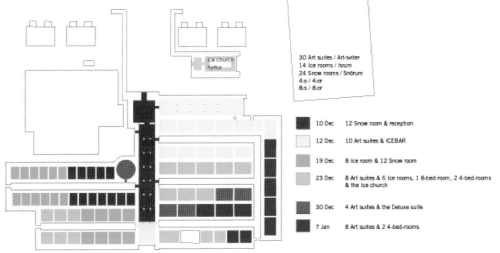

30 Art suites / Art-suiter
14 Ice rooms / Isrum
24 Snow rooms / Snörum
4:s / 4:or
8:s / 8:or

Ice church
Kyrka

	10 Dec	12 Snow room & reception
	12 Dec	10 Art suites & ICEBAR
	19 Dec	8 Ice room & 12 Snow room
	23 Dec	8 Art suites & 6 Ice rooms, 1 8-bed-room, 2 4-bed-rooms & the Ice church
	30 Dec	4 Art suites & the Deluxe suite
	7 Jan	8 Art suites & 2 4-bed-rooms

Architects:
Elenberg Fraser
Client:
Zacamoco
Completion:
2005

above:
Façade
below:
Exterior view from street

Falls Creek Huski Hotel

Built on a corner site, the Huski is a five level boutique apartment hotel, open for

both the winter and summer seasons at Falls Creek in the Victorian highlands. The design of the Huski is based on the study of snowflake geometry. Their pure yet complex patterns combined with the influence of Australian timber alpine huts and international alpine resorts provided the basis for the resulting architectural form. Radial in nature, the building responds to the delicate surrounding environment while utilizing the steep site of the building to maximize views of the Kiewa valley and Mt Spion Kopje, and allowing the scenery to penetrate every apartment. The modulated planes of the north façade emphasize the dynamic quality of the building both in terms of its layout plan and elevation. In contrast, the subtlety of the worn timber materials is calming and suggests a harmonious affinity with local building typologies.

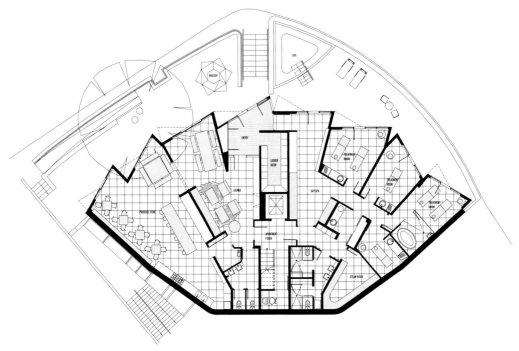

above left:
Living room with view
to the mountains
above:
Exterior view
mid:
Façade with view
of sundeck

below left:
Floor plan
below:
Hot tub on balcony with
view to mountains

Architects:
matteo thun &
partner
Client:
private
Completion:
2003

above:
Exterior view at night
below:
East side view

San Vigilio

Vigilius Mountain Resort

Reinterpreting traditional local wooden constructions, the building is made of stone, wood, clay and glass. Only the basement areas are made of reinforced concrete. The internal garden is planted with larch trees that create an authentic fragment of woodlands, which is incorporated into the architecture. All rooms face either east or west, featuring clay walls that absorb and then give off heat in winter and coolness in summer. The accessible landscaped roof helps prevent overheating while the large glass windows exploit solar energy, and adjustable shutters on the façade control the amount of shade. Everything is hermetically detailed, including controlled ventilation with heat recovery, the use of radiant panels on the inside and biomass heating to support nearby farming and safeguard the woodlands.

left:
Restaurant
above:
Interior
mid:
Seating at fireplace

below:
Ground floor plan

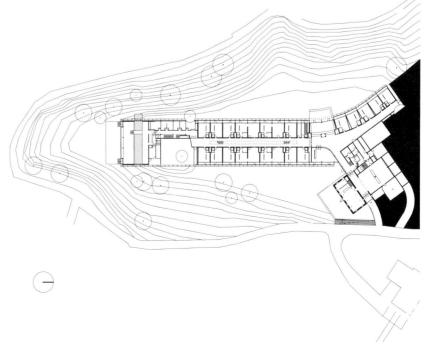

above:
Interior room
mid:
Lounge area with fireplace

below:
Spa area

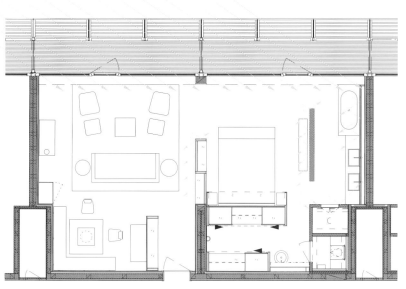

above:
Floor plan suite
below:
Sundeck

Architects:
Studio Architetto
Mario Botta
Client:
Tschuggen Grand
Hotel, Arosa,
Switzerland
Completion:
2006

above:
Glass bridge between
spa and hotel
below:
Snowy landscape

74

Arosa

Wellness Center
Tschuggen Bergoase

mountains. It is a place where there is a constant comparison between human beings and nature, emphasized by the powerful landscape, and where the ancestral fight between humans and mountains is evident. The site for the new Berg Oase structure is characterized, next to the great hotel, as a free space and park at the foot of the rear mountain. The architects' vision was to build apparently without a building, to assert the presence of the new through the newly added parts (e.g. artificial trees as a metaphor of nature), and to leave the great volume with the functional areas underground. The cover of the greened areas is staged as a pattern marked by geometrically arranged plants that arouse the visitor's curiosity.

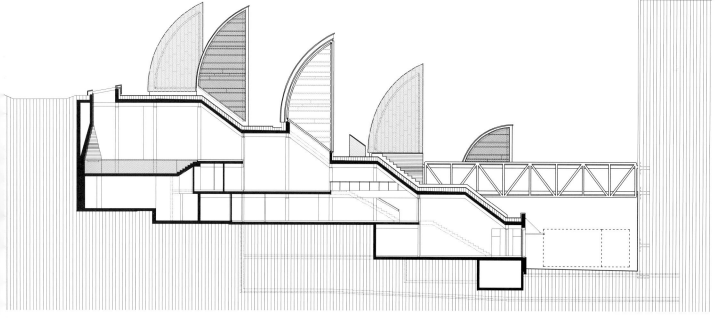

above left:
Relax area in the
'sauna world'
above:
Swimming pool
mid:
Swimming pool

below left:
Longitudinal section
below:
Detail curved wall of
swimming pool

Architects:
Gokhan Avcioglu &
GAD Architecture
Client:
Birtur & Irfan Kuris
Completion:
2008

above:
Exterior view of hotel suites
below:
Resort grounds

Golturkbuku

Kuum is conceived as a small settlement, nestled on a seafront bay, uniquely coexisting

Kuum Hotel
Spa & Residences

with the surrounding hillside topography. The clients wanted a design that looked and performed differently than what is normally expected in resorts for the Bodrum region. The different building typologies are organized to serve various programmatic needs, creating heterogeneous zones. The building shapes were also a consequence of the site's topographical ebbs and flows. To further heighten the heterogeneous effect, the architects focused on creating variations through the senses, in particular the visual, tactile and olfactory. The diversity in materials not only responds to the buildings' various programs, private and public spaces, etc., but also creates a visual and tactile richness. Thus the project creates a whole through differentiation.

above:
Hotel lobby at night
below:
Resort site plan

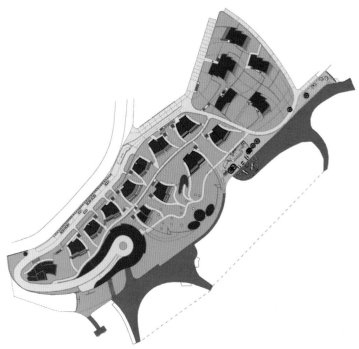

above:
Resort deck and bay
mid:
Hotel deck bar

below:
Interior of hotel suite

Architects:
ENOTA
Client:
Terme Olimia
Completion:
2006

above:
Interior room
below:
Lobby
right:
Detail façade

Podčetrtek

Wellness Hotel Sotelia was constructed to fill in the gap between two existing hotels,

Hotel Sotelia

both of which do not hide their different architectural origins. The new hotel does not try to repeat the style or materials of the nearby structures but rather clearly distances itself from the built environment and connects with its natural surroundings. In the design process, primary concern was to avoid an immense building mass, like the one suggested in the client's brief, which would have blocked the last remaining view of the forest. Instead, the volume was broken up into small units arranged in landscape-hugging tiers. As a result, the four-story 150-room building appears much lower and smaller than this description would suggest. The specific shape of the hotel was dictated by the folds in the landscape.

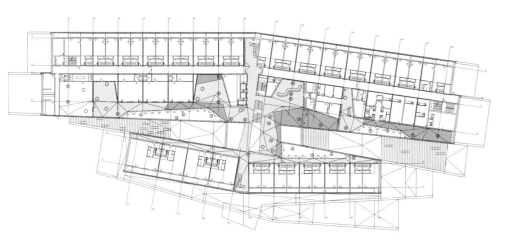

left:
Sundeck
above:
Floor plan
below:
Exterior view

Architect:
Werner Aschaber
Client:
One Hotel & Resorts
AG
Completion:
2008

above:
Grand suite, living area
below:
Wine tavern

Kitzbühel

Mountain Design Resort Hotel Kitzhof

Following extensive renovation and redecoration efforts, the hotel today presents itself with a very unique style and an innovative design of aged wood, glass, loden cloth, and modern furniture. The new image of the hotel is dominated by warm colors and natural materials. The design concept involves a large amount of glass and daylight. With great attention to details, the hotel combines stylish alpine flair with modern four-star comfort. The Kitzhof Suite offers a total of 170 square meters with two bedrooms, two bathrooms, a living area with an open fireplace, and an unparalleled panorama view across Kitzbühel. In the spa area, guests can enjoy a 15 x 5 meter indoor pool with special showers, relaxation zones and a winter garden, as well as a sauna landscape and fitness area.

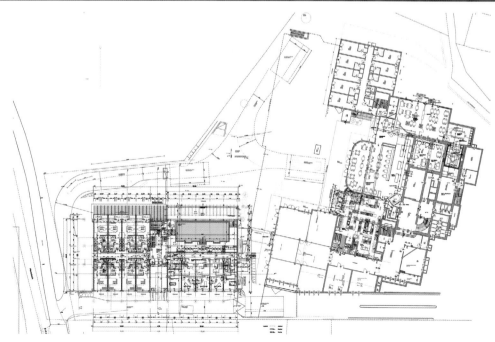

left:
Indoor pool
above:
Living area in small suite
mid:
Small suite bedroom

below left:
Ground floor plan
below:
Detail grand suite

designed

spaces

Architects:
Cabinet Vincent
BASTIE
Designer:
SandrineAlouf
Client:
The Five Hotel
Completion:
2008

above:
Interior
below:
Interior room

Paris

One by The Five

This room welcomes guests to the clouds. From the floor to the ceiling, the artist

Sandrine Alouf has given this private room a very unique layout concept – the unlimited sky and the lightly floating clouds. The bed is literally suspended in space, whilevarious optic fiber elements are reminiscent of the sun going down and the stars coming out. The optic fiber is the principal theme of the hotel's concept and its highlight. This silent and isolated cabinet room suggests different perfumes at guest's disposal, allowing them to adorn themselves with the most subtle fragrances. Each room aims to offer a different haven of peace, a real cocoon for every type of lover and leisure seeker. Each room offers its own fragrance, textures and, of course, optic fiber elements. The creation of a hotel consisting of a single suite has taken Philippe Vaurs one step further in his design work.

above:
View of room

below:
Skylight and interior

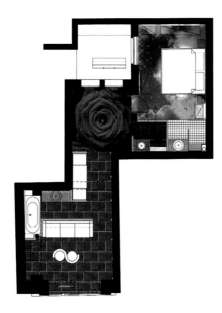

above:
Room plan
below:
Room

Architects:
JOI-Design
Innenarchitekten
GmbH
Client:
Dominic Müller
Completion:
2008

above:
One of the traditional rooms
below:
The traditional armchair

Düsseldorf

The current status quo of hotel interior design was presented at a special theme isle on the

Hogatec 2008

hogatec fair in September 2008. One type of room showcased was named 'Organic traces' – it highlighted the increased attention of our society on wellness and body and soul. A sculptural form in the middle of the room symbolized the fusion of different living areas with the bathroom. Another guestroom concept was called the 'Green room', which played with another very important topic – environmental sustainability. A green wall made of real plants acted as a reminder of the environment while purifying the air in the room. All other surfaces were made of natural materials as well. The third example, 'Art Deco' featured the return to the values of the past, which can remain topical in today's hectic lifestyle.

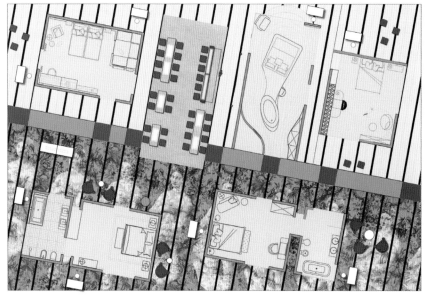

above left:
Modern green room
above:
Room with organic
structures

below left:
Ground floor plan
below:
Bathroom in the room

Architects:
P. Makridis +
Associates
Client:
Domotel S.A.
Completion:
2005

above:
Restaurant
below:
Entrance view
right:
Lobby

Thessaloniki

The project consisted of the conversion of a tobacco warehouse into a luxury hotel.

Les Lazaristes

The basic aims of the design were to combine spacious hotel rooms with efficient public spaces and hotel facilities, and to seamlessly weave together indoor and outdoor spaces. The two lower levels accommodate all public spaces and facilities, while the five upper levels contain the hotel's guestrooms. Metal canopies and grilles shade all windows and provide private balconies to the suites. The design of the interior combines beige marble with dark-varnished walnut wood for the public areas in which earthy colors and contemporary lines combine into a luxury environment. All rooms and public spaces are decorated with special pieces of art selected in collaboration with the most prominent cultural institutions of Thessaloniki.

above:
Seating area
right:
Restaurant

below:
Detail interior room

Architects:
Eventlabs GmbH
Designers:
21 international
artists
Client:
Brøchner-Hotels
Completion:
2005

above:
Restaurant
below:
Detail stairs
right:
Restaurant

Copenhagen

Hotel FOX

For the launch of the new Volkswagen Fox 21, international artists from the fields of graphic design, urban art and illustration turned Hotel Fox in central Copenhagen into the world's most exciting and creative lifestyle hotel. It offers its guests and visitors a total of 61 rooms created by 21 artist groups with the application of 1,000 ideas. Hotel Fox is truly an art hotel. Each room is a unique piece of art, which the hotel guests complement by staying, sleeping, working and moving around in. The rooms include an abundance of art, from wacky comical styles to strict graphic design, from fantastic street art and Japanese Manga to simply spaced out fantasies, with plenty of flowers, fairytales, friendly monsters, dreaming creatures, secrets vaults, and much more. The Hotel Fox reflects a truly new concept of mobility, travel and urban living culture.

above:
Room 106
mid:
Room 302

below:
Room 504

above:
Room 116
mid:
Room 214

below:
Room 309

Architects:
Kevin Hayes
Architects
Designers:
Alexander Lotersztain,
Derlot
Client:
KTG Managament
Completion:
2008

LIMES

above:
Foyer
below:
Front view
right:
Foyer

Brisbane

The Limes Hotel

intended look and feel, and paying heavy attention to the interiors, furniture, surfaces and finishes, as well as extending the design influence to the Limes' music and drinks list. The Limes façade was tangibly branded with a large-scale Limes logo, which is also found on details throughout the hotel lobby, rooms and rooftop bar and cinema. The bedroom design focused on the efficient use of space, prioritizing use and features. The material selection for the rooms was based on durability, maintenance and appeal. The result is a delicate balance of sophisticated warmth. The rooms feature custom Corian (by Dupont) kitchen benches and toilette vanities, Blackbutt timber bed heads, custom powder coat aluminum door handles, splash-back and floating bedside tables, Luna Textiles curtains and bathroom wall tiles by Bisazza.

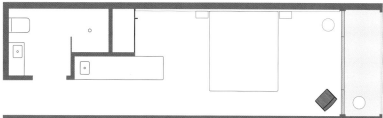

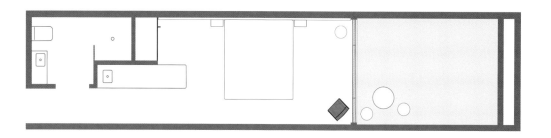

above left:
Bedroom
above:
Bedroom

below left:
Floor plans
below:
Bathroom

above:
Courtyard
right:
Breakfast at rooftop

below:
Rooftop

Architect:
Carmen Abad
Designers:
Antonio Miró,
Pilar Líbano
Client:
Mazarredo 77 S.L.
Completion:
2002

above:
Entrance hall and lobby
below:
Entrance view

114

Bilbao
MIRÓ HOTEL

Fashion designer Antonio Miró and Pilar Líbano were commissioned to create the first boutique hotel in Bilbao, with a contemporary functional design. The hotel´s location, between the Guggenheim and Fine Arts Museums, was important to the project. Art is present all over the hotel, whether in the hotel´s contemporary photography collection, or the hotel´s own original design. The first boutique hotel in the city, the Miró is exquisite in every sense of the word, combining functional design with personalized service. The 50 bedrooms are elegantly designed, well-decorated and furnished in line with the latest styles, to provide maximum comfort. Fine materials, maximum quality fabrics and up-to-date technology create an ideal space for rest and intimacy. The hotel offers a breakfast room while its bar is a meeting point for both local and international art lovers.

above:
Library
mid:
Entrance hall

below:
Ground floor plan

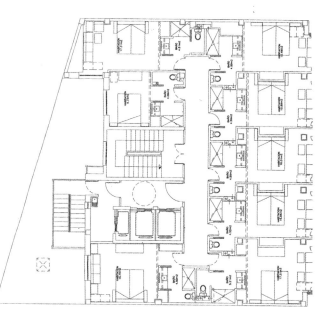

above:
Seating area
mid:
Interior room

below:
Spa area

Architects:
CorsoStaicoff
Designers:
CorsoStaicoff –
Interior Design;
Pappas Art - Art
Curation; Ditroen -
Graphic Art
Client:
Provenance Hotel
Group (Formerly
Aspen Hotel Group)
Completion:
2008

above:
Lobby
below:
Glass chandelier in lobby
right:
Front desk

Tacoma

Hotel Murano

cated boutique property, the design team looked to the flourishing local art community for influence. The Chihuly Bridge of Glass, by glass pioneer and Tacoma Native Dale Chihuly, and the Tacoma Glass Museum have been a major factor in distinguishing Tacoma from other cities. In the same manner, the design team wanted to link the hotel to the community using glass as its vehicle. The hotel collection includes established as well as up-and-coming artists from around the world. Art glass is integrated into everything, from the front desk to the entry door pulls. Each of the 21 guest floors is dedicated to an artist, featuring works displayed behind a customized etched glass wall engraved with the artist's commentary.

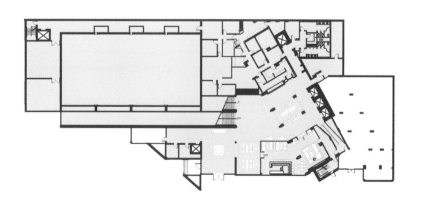

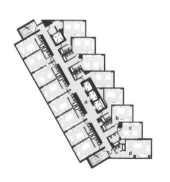

above left:
Glass art
below left:
Main lobby floor plan and
typical guestroom floor plan
above:
Guest corridor with
glass art wall
below:
Guestroom

WILLIAM MORRIS

Architect:
Simone Micheli
Architectural Hero
Client:
F.lli Barigliano
Completion:
2007

above:
View of the hall
below:
View of the hall separated
by the restaurant

Pisa

San Ranieri Hotel

In the heart of Tuscany, among antiques, artistic patrimonies, rich history, sea, and green

hills, the linear surfaces, washed out colors, fascinating transparencies and refined materials make Pisa the ideal setting for the implementation of a new visionary hospitality concept. This 'metropolitan design manifest' stimulates the visitors' senses, involving them in a unique and significant spatial connection. They are given a strong feeling of entering an illusionary world in which colors take control of emotions. The hotel's structure is surprising with its unique and exceptional crystal dome, which reflects the brilliant colors of the sunset, offering its guests a warm atmosphere, total comfort and total silence. The hotel features a number of differently styled venue halls and a unique restaurant – 'Squisitia' offering typical Tuscany cuisine in an exclusive setting.

above:
View of the elevators
and the hall
below:
View of the sinuous and
wrapping wall

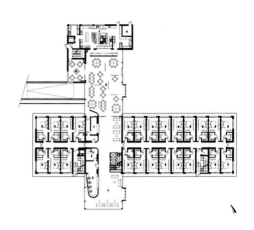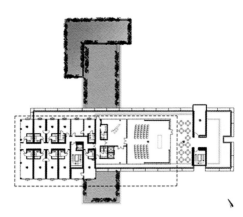

left:
View of the white
desk-warderobe
above:
Living area in the
black suite
mid:
Living area of suite

below:
Room view

Designers:
Delphine Buhro,
Michael Dreher
Client:
25hours Hotel
Company
Completion year:
2008

above:
Detail stairs
below:
Restaurant

Frankfurt

25hours Hotel by Levi's

25hours Hotel Company and the iconic jeans label Levi's. Featuring different shades of blue, the new design hotel in Frankfurt's city center is timeless and familiar like an old pair of blue jeans and has already been awarded European Hotel Property of the Year 2008. The furniture, lamps, carpeting, wallpaper and fabrics used on each floor were carefully selected by the local designers to evoke a different decade of the 20th century. The atmosphere ranges from a classic, crisp and clean to a casual cool stonewashed look. Apart from the 76 themed guestrooms, the hotel features a laid-back slow food restaurant, a roof deck terrace in the midst of the Frankfurt skyline, and a Gibson Music Session Room for hotel guests and local bands.

above:
1930ies interior room
mid:
Double room

below:
1960ies interior room

above:
1970ies twin room
mid:
Room number

below:
Reception desk

Architects:
Alexander Bernjus,
Hathumar Gisbertz
Designers:
Delphine Buhro,
Michael Dreher
Client:
25hours Hotel
Company
Completion year:
2006

above:
Living room
below:
Reception

Frankfurt

Goldman 25hours Hotel

vibrating East End, offering urban nomads and night owls an affordable and stylish place to stay. On seven floors with different themes, the 49 individually decorated guestrooms feature the stories of famous and infamous Frankfurt natives. High comfort basic equipment is combined with individual furniture items to create a unique atmosphere in each room. Upon arrival, visitors can choose whether they want to visit the Romans, Australia or a casino, rekindle childhood memories, wake up in the woods or dive for pearls in the Baltic Sea. The Hotel casually combines a multitude of valuable, surprising, sometimes ironic vintage objects and design classics with contemporary, clear-cut, customized furniture and hi-fi equipment. To fully understand this eclectic world, guests would have to visit the Goldman 25hours 49 times – at least.

above:
Interior room
mid:
Room 3.2
right:
Room 4.6

below:
Room 5.2

luxury

residences

Architects:
DP Architects
Designers:
Tai Lee Siang,
Chan Sui Him,
Tse Pek Mun
Client:
Far East Organization
Centre
Completion:
2004

above:
Swimming pool at night
below:
Saltwater Café – outdoor dining

Singapore

In complete contrast to its laidback and almost rustic setting in Changi Village, the

Changi Village Hotel

Changi Village Hotel was conceived as a hip and funky alternative to the more conventional hotels in downtown Singapore. Set in the eastern tip of the island, the Changi Village hotel underwent a comprehensive makeover. Spaces in the existing building, which is characterized by a triangular floor plan, were converted to new uses to support current and future hotel operations. Its facilities include a beautifully landscaped roof deck, fine dining establishments, a full spa and an infinity-edge pool set amidst tropical foliage, overlooking the Changi coastline and further off the Pulau Ubin and the South China Sea. The curvilinear façade of the building was also 'jazzed' up with the introduction of a series of multi-colored glass balconies, which offset the horizontal bands of glazing and white cladding, providing a refreshing facelift.

above:
Vau Wine bar

below:
Entrance at night

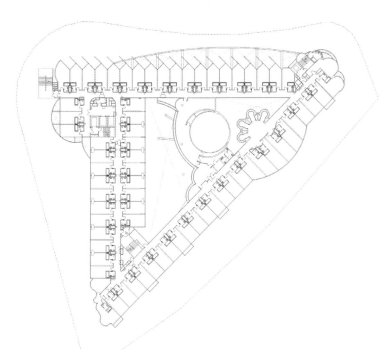

above:
Typical floor plan
below:
Royal Suite

Designers:
Tony Chi and
Associates
Completion:
2008

above:
Dining area
below:
Reception

Shanghai

Located on the top floors of the 492 meter high 101 floor-high Shanghai World Finan-

Park Hyatt

cial Center, which is also known as the 'Vertical Complex City', the Park Hyatt Shanghai towers above the Lujiazui business district in Pudong. Designed by Tony Chi, the hotel radiates an exclusive ambiance. From its dramatic entrance hall on the ground floor up to the reception on floor 87 and the Sky Residence on the 93rd floor, the hotel offers the perfect setting for business travelers and vacationers. On the 85th floor, the hotel offers its guests a water temple and an infinity pool next to a Tai-Chi square and a wellness studio. The Sky Residence on the 93rd floor is the world's highest restaurant and event venue. Each of the 174 guestrooms and suites of the hotel offers a panoramic view of the Huangpu river and Pudong.

above left:
Private dining
above:
Chairman Suite

below left:
Spa Water's Edge
below:
Hallway to conference room

Architect:
Maurice Giraud
Designers:
James Park
Associates
Client:
Taj Hotels Resorts
and Palaces
Completion:
2004

above:
Private sundeck with pool
below:
Exterior view

Wolmar
Taj Exotica Resort & Spa

The interior design predominately reflects a modern and eclectic style, set within a

framework of architecture that recalls French colonial-derived forms and rich lush tropical gardens. Contemporary furniture and decorative lighting effortlessly and casually combine with artifacts, antiques, and artworks inspired by natural objects and materials. Ultimately this modern and eclectic design approach aims to re-create the atmosphere and personality of a grand Mauritian home in a contemporary and modern context. The main reception building welcomes the guests with a series of carved timber screens using motifs from French Colonial, Indian, African, and Arab design. The materials used in the lobby have been kept to a restrained palette. Dark oak timber has been combined with the native Mauritian basalt stone. The library and meeting room lie off the main reception.

above:
Exterior spa area
below:
Spa area

above:
Interior room
below:
Detail room

left:
Bathtub in open room
above:
Restaurant

below:
Lounge

Architect:
Yousif Daoud
Al Sayegh
Client:
Six Senses
Resorts
& Spa
Completion:
2007

above:
Dining on the edge
below:
Private pool

152

Zighy Bay

Six Senses Hideaway

Positioned as the finest boutique resort in the Middle East, the Six Senses Hideaway Zighy

Bay establishes a new benchmark of luxury in the region. Located on the Musandam Peninsula of Oman, the resort is a 90 minutes drive from the gateway of Dubai. The dramatic setting, with mountains on one side and a 1.6 kilometers white sand beach at Zighy Bay, on the other, hosts 82 pool villas – all with butler service. The accommodations of Six Senses Hideaway Zighy Bay are a blend of the surrounding Omani traditional style with modern amenities that provide luxury local cultural themes. The resort has a spa, operated by the award-winning Six Senses Spa, with nine treatment rooms and two Arabian Hammams. Furthermore the resort includes three dining alternatives, including a dinner experience on the top of the mountain with a stunning view over Zighy Bay and the mountains.

above:
Dining on the edge
mid:
Wine tower cellar

below:
Juice bar in spa area

above:
The Retreat second
bedroom
below:
Spa area

Architects:
Foster + Partners
Designers:
United Designers,
London
Client:
Dolder Hotel AG
Completion:
2008

above:
General view
below:
Exterior view

156

Zurich
The Dolder Grand

Leading London architects Foster and Partners have combined the historic main building, dating from 1899, with the innovations of modern architecture. All the extensions added after 1899 have been demolished. Two new wings, the Spa Wing and the Golf Wing, curve around the fully restored main building in a fusion of past and future. Interior architects United Designers, also from London, have shaped new living spaces. Listed historic monument features as such as the Stone Hall in the main building and six of the bedrooms, have been faithfully restored to their original appearance. The Dolder Grand Spa is a unique, 4,000 square meter complex, in which architecture by Foster and Partners, interior design by United Designers and concept by the American spa expert Sylvia Sepielli combine to create an unique environment. Dynamic forms, selected materials and exciting light effects draw the visitor into an inspiring, totally sensual world.

above:
Bar
mid:
Pool in spa area

below:
Ground floor plan

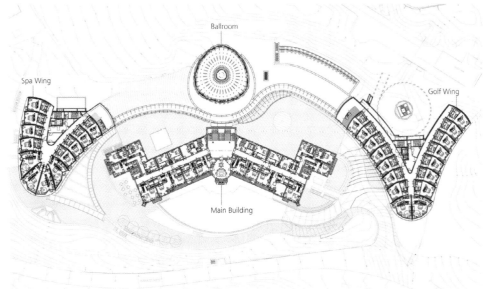

Ballroom

Spa Wing

Golf Wing

Main Building

above:
Lobby
mid:
Junior suite

below:
Junior suite

Architects:
Studio Gaia, Inc.
Designer:
Ilan Waisbrod
Client:
Starwoods
Completion:
2004

above:
Concierge desk at lobby
left:
Lobby seating area
right:
Lobby lounge

Seoul

W Seoul Walkerhill

Architecture and interior emphasize the purity of shapes and forms over ornamental

décor. The aim of the design was to evoke emotional states by appealing to the senses, often in dramatic ways. A striking entrance invites guests into the living room, where clear rectangular structural components and different seating areas are highlighted by custom-made furniture. On one floor, the retail area is a colorful candy shop structured by wood partitions, that are used for displays; while in the elevators one can hold on to lighted hand rails similar to old subway cars. In order to give returning guests a different experience, the hotel features 4 different room types. Each is specially designed with curtains, diverse beds and bold textures to offer relaxation and inspiration. The hotel's simple, yet striking colors and stunning bathrooms offer a fresh contemporary look every time.

161

left:
Bar
above:
VIP lounge
mid:
DJ platform /
dance platform

below:
Seating area

above:
Spa suite with shower room
mid:
Spa suite living room

below:
Spa suite bathroom

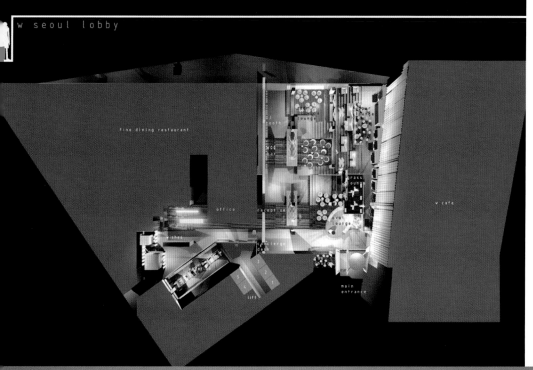

above:
Floor plan
below:
Presidential suite bedroom

Architects:
Jestico + Whiles
Client:
More London
Development
Completion:
2007

above:
Exterior view
below:
Lobby

166

London

Hilton Tower Bridge

The 246-room Hilton Tower Bridge is located in the heart of More London, a business district on the southern bank of The Thames. The outer design of the hotel consits of three interconnected 'strips' combining the style and texture of the Tooley Street historic Conservation Area and More London's contemporary silver and glass-dominated commercial buildings. The inner strips are clad in limestone-colored terracotta panels. At the lower levels, they turn into horizontal terracotta tiles set next to each other with varying densities. The hotel interior features natural materials, textures and colors, which are contrasted with juicy colors and enhanced by perfect lighting. A frosted glass box of the conference room cantilevers over the main site axis, and is stained with deep, saturated colored light to sign the hotel from afar.

above:
Seating area
below:
Lounge

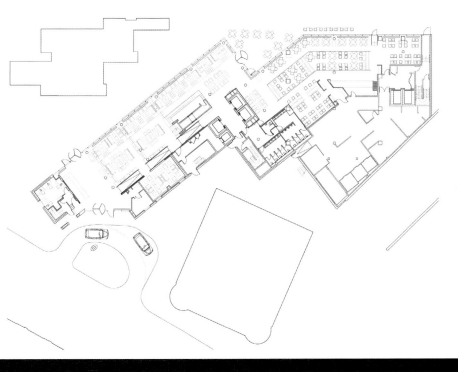

above:
Ground floor plan
below:
Bedroom

Architects:
Jestico + Whiles
Client:
Jemstock Properties
Completion:
2006

above:
Bar
below:
Reception

London
Hilton Canary Wharf

The Hilton London Canary Wharf hotel is located at the heart of Canary Wharf's bus-tling business, café and shopping scene. The 14-floor 286-room Hilton hotel is part of the Discovery Dock West development of this area. The interior was designed by Jestico + Whiles. The ground floor of the hotel consists of an uninterrupted space compromising reception, lobby bar and restaurant. Pools of light, rich color highlights and contrasting textures emphasize the area's features and define its different zones. The simple natural materials, including honed stone, lucent pond-green glass, shimmering mesh, and a rough wall of rust and multi-colored riven slate, create a cool, tranquil refuge within this busy commercial center.

above:
Lobby
below:
Lounge

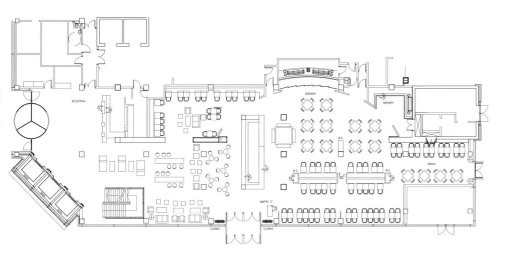

above:
Ground floor plan
below:
Interior room

wellness

islands

Architects:
P. Makridis +
Associates
Client:
Chatzikonstantinou
Bros. S.A.
Completion:
2008

above:
Exterior view at night
below:
Detail spa area

Alexandroupoli
Alexander Beach Hotel & Convention Center

Alexander Beach Hotel is a newly renovated spa hotel in Alexandroupoli. The rooms

SAUNA MASSAGE

were enlarged and enhanced by en-suite outdoor lounging terraces with private swimming pools. The interior was partially covered with oak paneling, creating a warm and hospitable feeling. The abstract handling of the design in combination with the unique style of furnishings bestows an additional nuance to the sophisticated, cosmopolitan atmosphere. Careful attention was given to the arrangement of the lighting, often employing indirect sources of light, for a more dramatic ambiance that enhances the warmth of the employed materials. The renovation included the creation of a wellness center with special facilities for warm and cold-water treatments that offer plenty of opportunity for physical and spiritual well being.

above:
Spa area
mid:
Bathroom
above right:
Interior room

below:
Detail room
below right:
Floor plan

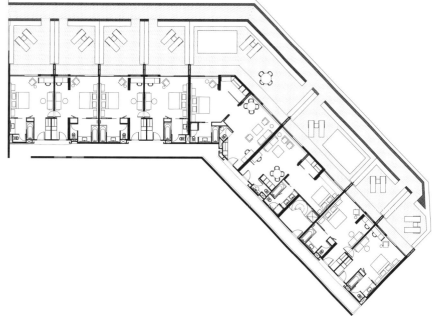

Architects:
Pascal Arquitectos
Client:
Inmobiliaria
Interpress
Completion:
2004

above:
Panoramic view
below:
The lower part of the building
holds the lobby

180

Mexico City

Sheraton Centro Histórico Hotel

tectos, is located in downtown Mexico City across the 'Alameda Central', along Avenida Juarez next to the 'Palacio de Bellas Artes', 'Casa de los Azulejos' and the 'Torre Latinoamericana' at the main entrance of Mexico City's historical downtown district. The architectural firm was in full charge of the entire architectural and interior design. The hotel has been constructed with 26 levels. It offers 464 rooms, a convention center, boutiques, restaurants, cafeterias, spa and a heliport. This is the first high scale project accomplished in Mexico City's historic downtown in forty years and after the 1985 earthquakes. The historically designed entrance along Avenida Juarez was required by the National Institute of Anthropology and History.

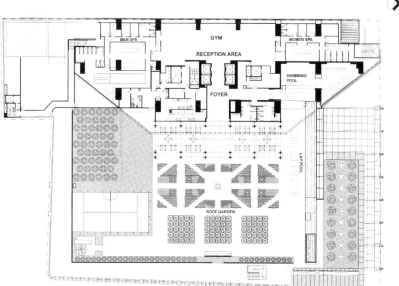

above left:
Swimming pool area
above:
Reception
mid:
Entrance men spa

below left:
Plan of spa and roof garden
below:
Bedroom

Architects:
Matias Gonzalez &
Rodrigo Searle
Designers:
Alexandra Edwards &
Carolina del Piano
Client:
Asesorías e
Inversiones Katari S.A.
Completion:
2008

above:
Detail exterior at night
below:
Interior view of spa

184

San Pedro de Atacama
Tierra Atacama Hotel & Spa

For environmental reasons, the whole hotel was built on a platform, leaving the existing historic ground untouched. The surrounding land, neglected for many years, was returned to its agricultural state and planted again with grains, fruit trees, herbs and flowers native to the area. The difficulty of building in a remote location led to a lighter style of building material, reducing the use of various materials such as cement, moldings and water – all scarce in the desert environment. Local labor was used to build walls made of stone and rammed earth, which protect the exteriors and blend with the surroundings. Finally, the setting consists of an extensive and diverse landscape, which is gathered in parts in frames to mark special views, and successive patios which range from very open spaces, passing through intermediate areas with gardens, water and fig trees, to the most private, shady and protected space for each occupant.

above:
View on landscape
mid:
Spa rest area

below:
Exterior view with
swimming pool

above:
Fireplace
mid:
Dining room

below:
Site and floor plan

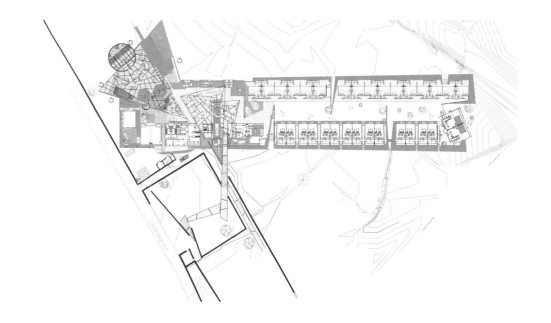

Architect:
Hugo Demetz –
demetzarch
Designers:
Hugo & Hanspeter
Demetz
Client:
Le Fay Resorts
Completion:
2008

above:
Main building at night
below:
Main building from south

188

Gargnano

Lefay Resort & Spa Lago di Garda

Lefay Resort & SPA Lago di Garda is a five-star wellness hotel with 100 rooms, build in a extraordinary location. The architecture indicates that it is near to nature, eco-friendly, well integrated in the environment, made of local materials, and equipped with advanced eco-techniques. The hotel is composed of a main building that contains the public rooms and 2-story bedroom-buildings connected by corridors. The buildings are dispersed among the hills and terraces. As a result, the entire size of the resort is never visible, while the wonderful view and nature are predominant. The resort includes outdoor and indoor pools with infinity effects and a saltwater lake in the cavern. The roof restaurant is built with a photovoltaic glass vault. The alternative energy concept of the resort includes 80% self-generated power.

189

above:
Fireplace of
iron and stone
below:
View from bathroom

190

above:
Site plan
below:
View of
Lago di Garda

above:
Sauna area
mid:
Caligo Sauna
right:
Sauna area

below:
Lady sauna

Architects:
Architrave Design and
Planning
Client:
Banyan Tree Group
Completion:
2007

above:
Private dining
below:
Royal pool villa

Al Areen

Banyan Tree Desert Spa and Resort

trend of opulent Arab interiors dressed in rich russet gold and orange tones. Presenting a majestic silhouette on the Arab horizon, the hotel is a mix of Middle Eastern art and contemporary design. Banyan Tree Al Areen opened its doors in April 2007 as the only all-villa, private swimming pool and jet-pool resort in the Middle East, the world's most extensive and luxurious spa and hydrothermal garden, with three international restaurants, a complete body wellness center and the award-winning Banyan Tree Gallery. Banyan Tree Al Areen presents a total of 78 luxuriously appointed villas; 56 one-bedroom Desert Pool Villas, of 400 square meter each; as well as 22 two-bedroom Royal Pool Villas each spanning 740 square meter and featuring private open-air swimming and jet pools, over-sized infinity bath tubs and sprawling master bedrooms.

left:
Vertigo lounge
above:
Hydrothermal pool
mid:
Indoor lap pool

below:
Outdoor freeform pool

above:
Bedroom
mid:
Interior bathroom
right:
Private villa with
indoor pool

below:
Floor plan

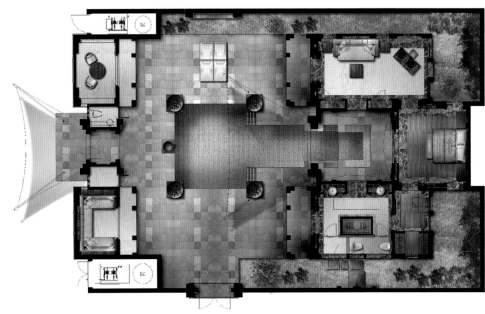

Architects:
Jestico + Whiles
Client:
Orco Property Group
Completion:
2007

above:
Bird's eye view on the hotel
below:
Lounge area and bar at night

Hvar

Hotel Adriana

The deluxe four-star Adriana Hvar Marina Hotel is a striking addition to Hvar's water-front promenade. Together with a luxurious spa and outdoor treatment terraces, the hotel is Croatia's first member of the 'Leading Small Hotels of the World' group. The Adriana's appeal is the sophisticated simplicity of its architecture which is carried through and exploited in the interior design concept. Behind the simple, elegant sandstone façade with its grid of bedroom windows featuring narrow sliding shutters is a comfortable restaurant and lobby space, a ground floor lobby bar, a rooftop bar and lounge, 59 guestrooms and suites, and a fourth floor saltwater pool. The ultra modern bedrooms with their mix of versatile materials, clever use of available space, and selective use of color provide a comfortable refuge.

above:
Outdoor massage cabana
below:
Floor plan

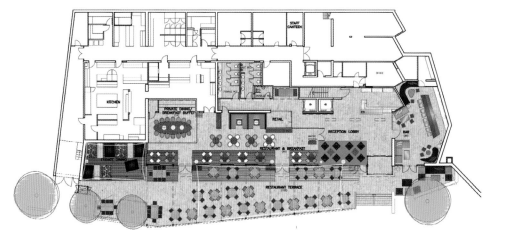

above:
Lobby bar
mid:
Rooftop heated saltwater
pool

below:
Bedroom

urban

hideouts

Architects:
Tassilo Bost / bost
group berlin
Client:
Deutsche Interhotel
Holding GmbH &
Co.KG
Completion:
2006

above:
Bar Spagos
below:
Lobby with oversized
glass cabinet

Leipzig

bost group berlin completely renovated the 4-star business hotel Radisson SAS, Leipzig.

Radisson SAS

The eye catcher in the lobby is a colorful illuminated glass cabinet. Cream-colored over-sized lounge sofas contrast with red cushions and brown leather chairs. The hotel bar features scattered bronze tones with red dashes. In addition to its centerpiece, a high legged table, the bar has a lounge area and a separated booth veiled by illuminated curtains. In the adjacent bistro, the walls are covered with speckled bronze coating. Darkly tinted lumbers give the room a smooth atmosphere. Due to a newly installed glass façade, the spacious guest-rooms are flooded with light, while a transparent shower dissolves the classic room structures. As a special effect, in the corridors the room numbers are cast onto the doors by light projections.

above:
Restaurant
mid:
Junior suite

below:
Ground floor plan

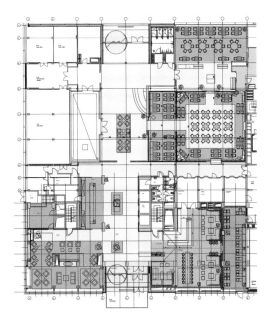

above:
Guestroom sleeping area

below:
Bathroom with sealife
athmosphere

Architects:
Studio architetto
Daniele Beretta
Designers:
matteo thun &
partners
Client:
DHD srl
Completion:
2006

above:
Reception area
below:
Lobby

210

Milan

The architect's concept trans-
lates his catch-phrase of 'fluid
design' into tangible reality.

Nhow Hotel Milan

He has converted the classical railway shed factory building into a refreshingly spacious hotel inspired by the
airy roominess of the classical American loft. At the same
time, he maintained the es-
sentials of the building's
industrial roots and added
eclectic public areas, lounges,
restaurants and bars with a
stylishly young atmosphere
that combines street art and
the finest of design elements.
On the outside, the entire
building is encased in an im-
posing grey structure with a
pattern of generous windows.
Inside, the guestrooms ema-
nate industrial chic conveyed
with taste and style combined
with a refreshing sense of individuality. All rooms are in-
geniously furnished with mod-
ular elements used in a
different fashion every time.

left:
Dining area
above:
Bathroom

below:
Sketch of superior bedroom

Architects:
Jan Kleihues,
Kleihues + Kleihues
Client:
Grothe Immobilien
Projektierungs KG
Completion:
2005

above:
Suite
below:
Lobby
right:
Front Elevation
Joachimstaler Straße,
Augsburger Straße

Berlin

Hotel Concorde

Consistently and continuously styled inside and outside, including the minutest detail, the towering 18-floor corner building is stacked along its tapered street-facing sides. The façade is covered in Kirchheim shell limestone. The exterior lines are continued on the inside with clear shapes, warm colors and elegant furnishings. The lines are reflected on the reception counter, the walls, the screen-style division walls, and the hand rail of the lobby. The concept is then continued as an individual strip in the public areas, to be dissolved in the rooms into a spatial three-dimensional meander visible in parts of the furniture and the handles of the sliding doors. The reception, lobby, elevator lobby, bar and restaurant areas are smoothly interlaced, yet maintain their own identity due to their mirror symmetry which clearly identify them as independent areas.

left:
Suite Blanche
above:
Meander Suite
mid:
Suite Dolomit

below:
Meander Suite

Architects:
Gert Wingårdh /
Wingårdh
Arkitektkontor AB
Designers:
Gert Wingårdh, Per
Söderberg, Vanja
Knocke, Cecilia Ström,
Interior: Lena Arthur
Client:
Bantorget Invest AB,
Arthur Buchardt
Completion:
2008

above:
Reception and lobby
below:
Terrace and spa

Stockholm

Like two pointed scissor blades, the building jabs the air between Norra Bantorget

Clarion Hotel Sign

and the Central Station shunting yard. One blade leans slightly outwards towards the piazza, as if honing the edge of its corner. Due to the often hazardous transport operations in the shunting yard, no windows were installed on the other blade, where instead free play is given to the horizontal striation that encircles the building. Black granite provides the façade with a rustic massiveness on the ground and an ethereal buoyancy skywards. Glazing and polished stone mirror the verdure on the street side. With its double-headroom ground floor and an entrance extending towards the piazza, the hotel complements the public character of the setting, while at the same time its architecture adds an independent element. The strong graphics and edges of the façades are repeated in the interior.

above:
Interior suite
above right:
Sundeck

below right:
Floor plan
below:
Breakfast and dining room

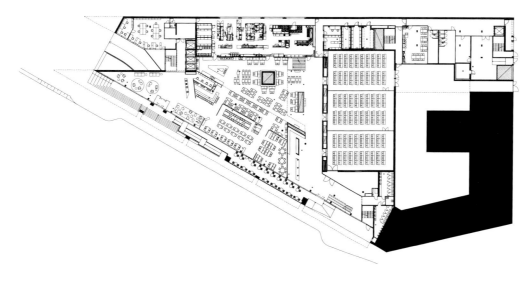

Architect:
Kim Utzon Arkitekter
Client:
Arp-Hansen Hotel
Group
Completion:
2006

above:
Reception desk
below:
Bar
right:
Atrium

Copenhagen

The hotel is located near the harbor in Copenhagen, surrounded by water. Towering

Copenhagen Island

eight stories high, the lobby building connects the two six-story wings with their 325 rooms, conference facilities and a restaurant, overlooking the harbor. The hotel opened its doors in the summer of 2006 welcoming its guests to a one-of-a-kind experience. Ultra modern qualities characterize the entire hotel. In addition to the 325 air conditioned rooms, equipped with free wireless internet and flat screen television, the hotel also encompasses a fitness center and, not the least, an exciting restaurant. Appropriately named The Harbor, it offers diners a stunning view across the harbor. Copenhagen Island's fantastic architecture and many luxurious facilities give the hotel a completely unique atmosphere that distinguishes it from other hotels.

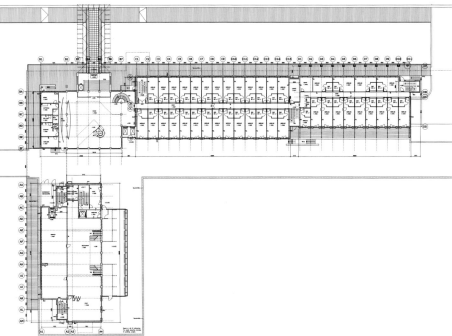

above left:
Dining area
above:
Restaurant
mid:
Interior room

below left:
Floor plan
below:
Interior room

Architects:
Edgar Stoffersen with
Katrin Wagner
Designers:
Jordan Mozer and
Associates Limited
Client:
Kreye and Partner
Completion:
2005

above:
Restaurant
below:
Seating area

226

Hamburg

The design was inspired by
the old foundry shapes of the
cast iron objects that were

East Hotel

once produced at this location,
by the contemporary cross-
breeding of Eastern and Western cultures, and by the con-
viction that public spaces
should have strong idiosyn-
cratic personalities and an internal logic similar to a dream
or a poem. The design elements borrow from these in-
spirations – cooled molten/
cast forms, hot fat raindrops,
an enlarged and simplified
Thai cowbell, the colors of
Indian spices along with flowers and silks, high-contrast
forms and materials, unex-
pected shifts of scale and form,
as well as elements that are
at once familiar and strange.
The interior architecture
blends remnants of the old
foundry with forms imagined
in paintings and sculptures
created by a mixture of com-
puter technology and traditional building techniques.

above:
Detail stairs
right:
Interior room

below:
First floor plan

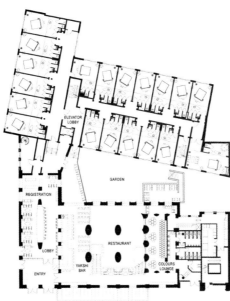

Architects:
Thomas Lau;
Mark Hendrik Blieffert
Designer:
Sibylle von Heyden
Client:
Gastwerk Hotel GmbH
& Co. KG
Completion year:
2007

above:
Exterior view
below:
Bar
right:
Lounge

Hamburg

25hours Hotel

design trends and affordable style. The outstanding flexibility of the public areas is at the core of the hotel's young design concept. The ground floor consists of a lobby, restaurant, living room and meeting facilities, which can all be easily changed into an expansive multi-purpose venue for large parties and functions. The 104 guestrooms offer a cheerful design mix, borrowing elements primarily from the 1960s and 1970s with an abundance of beaming white. The original concept of the 3meta design team was enhanced in 2006 by local interior designer Sibylle von Heyden – the addition of the playful 25hours guesthouse, featuring its own pink kitchen, ideally complements the overall style of this uncomplicated hotel.

above:
Detail room
mid:
Interior hotel room

below:
Bedroom

above:
Seating area with fireplace
mid:
Lounge

below:
Conference room

Architects:
Concrete Architectural
Associates
Designers:
Graphic design and
visuals:
KesselsKramer
Client:
CitizenM
Completion:
2008

above:
Detail façade
below:
Lobby

Schiphol

CitizenM Hotel

Two big glass cylinders contain the shower and the toilet, while a small Corian cylinder contains the washbasin and extra storage space. The shower consists of a fixed half cylinder and two quarter cylinder sliding doors, all made of transparent glass. The building is a black metal box dominated by the bulging glass windows of the rooms. The various depths of the aluminum frames and the angled glass provide the rigid façade with an individual twist. The big glass windows on the ground floor are placed inside the building, creating a natural transfer between inside and outside and exposing the living rooms and lobby space to the street. As an extension of this dynamic interior, a red colored glass box marks the entrance. Two huge works of art, printed on pvc mesh fabric, are placed on the façade. The work of a local artist, they will travel from one hotel façade to the other within a few years.

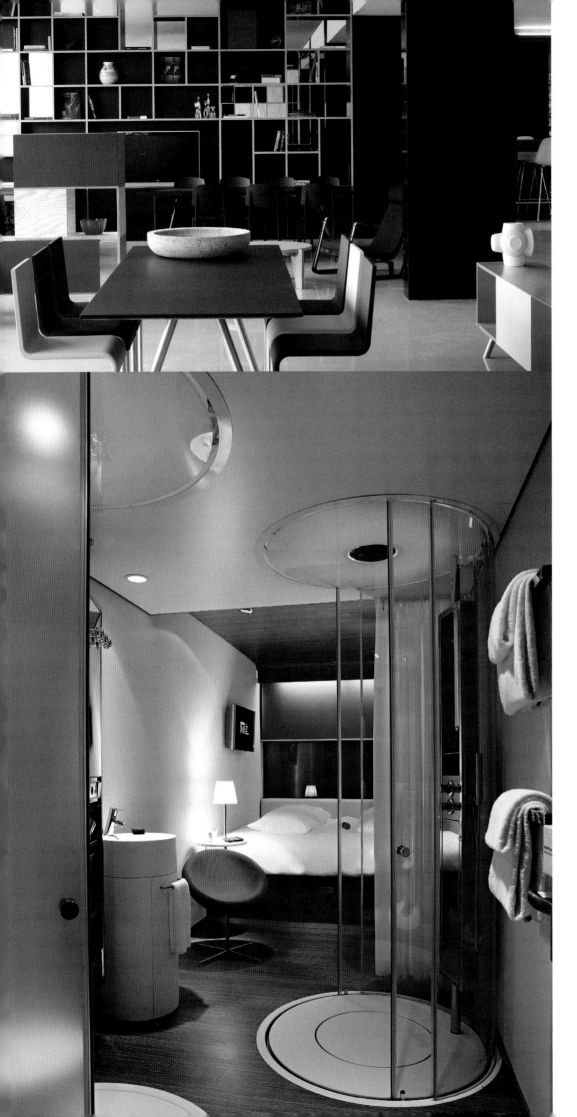

above:
Lobby view
above right:
Room view

below:
Shower
below right:
Ground floor plan

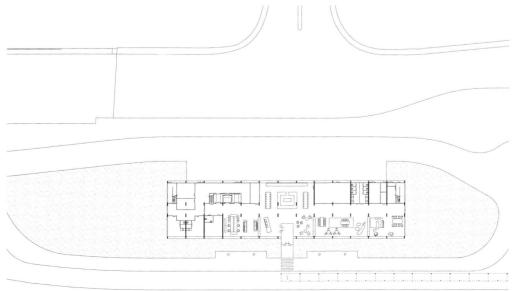

noord

countryside

hotels

Architects:
Roberto Gallo assisted
by Alessandra
Pappalardo
Clients:
Emanuela Marino –
Gareth Shaughnessy
Completion:
2006

above:
View of hotel entrance
below:
Pool
right:
Restaurant

Syracuse

Caol Ishka Hotel is located on the bank of the Anapo river, only two kilometers

Caol Ishka Hotel – Zafferano Bistrot

from Syracuse's historical center. Contemporary design meets the charm of an old Sicilian Masseria: in a warm mix, materials, designer furniture and antique pieces have all been blended into a rustic environment. The garden consists of a wide lawn beside the pool giving way to the surrounding nature with bamboo, wild grass and spontaneous vegetation. Whereas the outside exhibits a traditional feel, the inside features white and natural oak beam roofs that alternate with white ceilings; warm colors for walls and floorings in colored resin and hardwoods. Bathrooms are spacious with designer basins and large walk-in showers. Oversized doors have been crafted by local artisans with various finishes: bisazza mosaics, mirrors, and gold leaf.

above:
Reading room and
internet point
mid:
Black marble table by
Eero Saarinen

below:
Floor plan

above:
Superior room
mid:
Deluxe room

below:
Site plan

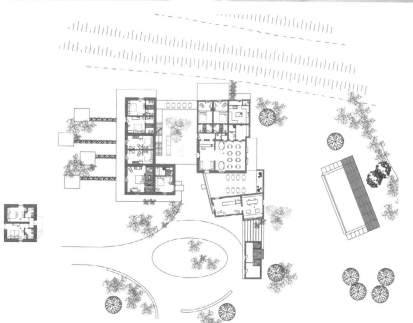

Architect:
Germán del Sol
Client:
Inmobiliaria Mares
del Sur Ltda.
Completion:
2006

above:
Exterior view at night
below:
Exterior view
right:
Lounge

244

Puerto Natales

Hotel Remota is inspired by the buildings used for the work carried out indoors on

Hotel Remota

sheep farms because of the wind and cold. A Latin American cultural tradition is to place architecture in the middle of nature, without the mediation of streets or cities, to provide people with an inspiring place to live in awe of the surrounding vastness. The empty central courtyard introduces the extensiveness of Patagonia to the core of the hotel. It is surrounded by two guestroom buildings, along with public areas and service buildings. Three wooden corridors that cross the courtyard connect the buildings. Their wooden walls constitute the fourth border of the courtyard, while their roofs form a close horizon that lets one appreciate the vastness beyond. The wild grass of the Patagonian plains is left to grow wild all around the premises and also cover the roofs of buildings.

above:
Lounge
mid:
View from second floor

below:
Elevations

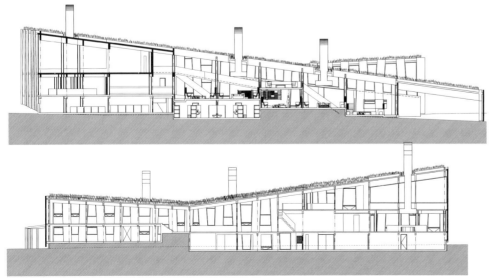

above:
Interior living room
mid:
Bedroom

below:
Bedroom

Architect:
Sebastian Irarrazaval
Clients:
Olivier Potart, Ana
Ibáñez, Hernán Jofré
Completion:
2006

above:
Exterior view
below:
Lobby
right:
Hammock in lobby

248

Puerto Natales
Indigo Patagonia Hotel

To allow the exploration of the entire building in a continuous way, an inner circulation path was created evolving from a soft ramp to a system of staircases and from corridors to bridges, allowing horizontal and vertical movement to become an orchestrated choreography within the building. The design was sensitive of the site and its provincial character, therefore using materials already present in the town to design a simple volume combined with a systematic rhythm of windows. To radically differentiate the intimate space of the guest bedrooms from the monumental space of public areas, a horizontal strata made of pine was created, incorporating all usable surfaces in the rooms. In contrast, the public spaces mainly consist of vertical spaces in which a huge shutter or curtain made of eucalyptus bars is always present.

left:
Restaurant with drop-light
above:
Wooden construction

below:
Lounge

above:
View to outdoor pool
mid:
Spa area
above right:
Bedroom

below:
Spa area
below right:
Detail bathroom

Architect:
Germán del Sol
Client:
Salfa SA
Completion:
2006

above:
Exterior view
below:
Hallway
right:
Sundeck with panoramic view

254

San Pedro de Atacama

Built on the Ayllú (neighborhood) de Larache in San Pedro de Atacama, the Explora en

Hotel Explora en Atacama

Atacama resembles a small town built around three patios. The rooms are arranged along corridors opening to a patio. The corridors meet in the main building, crossed by two ample passages; the Pasaje del Sol and the pasaje del Agua. The hotel is positioned around a rocky elevation, raised one meter above the natural level of the land, providing an extensive view of the surrounding pastures. The ground level of the public areas is four meters high, offering a view of the horizon in which the vastness of Atacama appears in all its splendor. In search of a balance between the direct light of the sun of Atacama and the shades, some areas have been made of wooden grates, while the walls throw shadows on each other, by the trembling movement of their form.

above:
Hotel room
mid:
Exterior view

below:
Courtyard

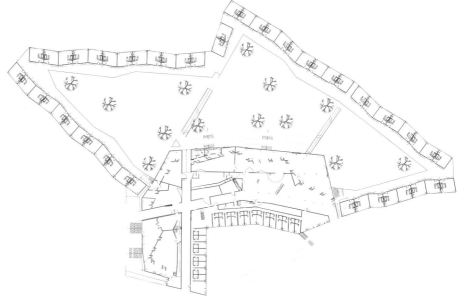

Architects:
Architrave Design and
Planning
Client:
Banyan Tree Group's
Completion:
2006

above:
General view
below:
Villa with outdoor pool

Yunnan
Banyan Tree Lijiang

Located 2,000 meters above sea level in the heart of China, Banyan Tree Lijiang is 15 min-

utes way from the historical town of Dayan, a UNESCO-designated World Heritage Site, and 40 minutes away from Lijiang Airport. Banyan Tree Lijiang offers 55 stunning single-story villas, all facing northeast with breathtaking views of the legendary Jade Dragon Snow Mountain. The villas are spacious, each measuring at least 350 square meters, with private gardens and heated outdoor jet pools or plunge pools. Banyan Tree Lijiang also includes three courtyards and a series of interconnected canals, copying the original imperial style. Inspired by the local Naxi culture, pink stone, grey Naxi bricks and traditional red clay roof tiles were used for construction. All buildings bear signature Naxi-style curved roofs.

above:
Inner courtyard with pond
below:
Garden site

above:
Exterior view of villa
below:
View to bedroom

Architects:
Habita Architects
Designer:
Khun Saran
Soontornsuk
Client:
Six Senses
Resorts & Spa
Completion:
2007

above:
Dining room
below:
Exterior view of bar

Koh Yao Noi

Six Senses Hideaway

Koh Yao Noi is a picturesque island in Thailand's Phang Nga Bay – the unique natural environment setting for the 24-acre Six Senses Hideaway Yao Noi, which exemplifies the Six Senses Hideaway philosophy of redefining experiences from arrival to departure. The natural vegetation and tropical landscaping provide privacy and allow glorious views over Phang Nga Bay. The resort has 54 private pool villas, plus the Hilltop Reserve, and the Retreat; all representing an uncompromised high standard of luxury. The attention to detail and focus on the nature and characteristics of the destination reinforces Six Senses' commitment to the environment. Each villa has its own infinity-edged pool with a sundeck. The dining room features a glass floor with a creek meandering underneath, while the living room presents a wide range of world cuisine, with an emphasis on Thai dishes.

below:
Master bedroom

above left:
Spa Bathroom
above:
Bathroom of pool villaa
mid:
Spa treatment room

below:
Pool site

above:
Juice bar at spa area
below:
Sitting area at pool villa

above:
Seaside
below:
Dining room

Portraits
Architects

Sandrine Alouf

contact@sandrinealouf.com
www.sandrinealouf.com
► 92

Andromeda International SRL

Miotti 16
30141 Murano (VE)
Italy
T +39.041.73 66 74
F +39.041.527 44 53
info@andromedamurano.it
www.andromedamurano.it
► 22

Tassilo Bost / bost group berlin

Danckelmannstraße 9
14059 Berlin
Germany
T +49.30.308 30 70
F +49.30.30 12 11 17
info@bost-group.com
www.bost-group.com
► 206

Studio Architetto Mario Botta

Via Ciani 16
6904 Lugano
Switzerland
T +41.91.972 86 25
F +41.91.970 14 54
mba@botta.ch
www.botta.ch
► 74

concrete architectural associates bv

Rozengracht 133 III
1016 LV Amsterdam
The Netherlands
T +31.20.520 02 00
F +31.20.520 02 01
pers@concreteamsterdam.nl
www.concreteamsterdam.nl
► 234

CorsoStaicoff

338 SE Martin Luther King Blvd
Portland, OR 97214
USA
T +1.503.231 92 22
F +1.503.231 92 66
heather@corsostaicoff.com
www.corsostaicoff.com
► 118

Hugo Demetz – demetzarch

Burgfriedenkapelle
39042 Brixen
Italy
T +39.0472.83 15 23
F +39.0472.20 71 89
demetzarch@libero.it
www.demetzarch.com
► 188

**Derlot Pty. Ltd.,
Alexander Lotersztain**

info@derlot.com
www.derlot.com
► 108

DP Architects Pte Ltd

6 Raffles Boulevard
#04-100 Marina Square
Singapore 039594
Singapore
T +65.63 38 39 88
F +65.63 37 99 89
dparchitects@dpa.com.sg
www.dpa.com.sg
► 38

Elenberg Fraser

374 George st, Fitzroy
Melbourne Victoria 3065
Australia
T +61.394 17 28 55
F +61.394 17 28 66
mail@e-f.com.au
www.e-f.com.au
► 64

ENOTA

Poljanska cesta 6
1000 Ljubljana
Slovenia
T +38.61.438 67 40
F +38.61.438 67 45
enota@enota.si
www.enota.si
► 82

Foster + Partners

Riverside 22 Hester Road
London SW11 4AN
United Kingdom
T +44.20.77 38 04 55
F +44.20.77 38 11 07
press@fosterandpartners.com
www.fosterandpartners.com
► 156

Roberto Gallo

Via Sirio 19 Fontane Bianche
96100 Siracusa
Italy
T +39.33 35 75 48 16
robertgal7@hotmail.com
► 240

Matias Gonzalez & Rodrigo Searle

Juan Agustin Alcalde 2876
Vitacura, Santiago de Chile
Chile
T +56.24.26 90 30
F +56.24.26 90 26
fg@fgarquitectos.cl
www.fgarquitectos.cl
► 184

Jestico + Whiles

1 Coburg Street
NW1 2HP London
United Kingdom
T +44.20.7380 0382
F +44.87.0622 0732
jw@jesticowhiles.com
www.jesticowhiles.co.uk
► 166, 170, 200

Sebastian Irarrazaval

General O'brien 2458
Vitacura 7630000
Santiago de Chile
Chile
T +56.2.245 62 52
sebastian@sebastianirarrazaval.com
www.sebastianirarrazaval.com
► 248

JOI Design GmbH Innenarchitekten

Medienpark [k]ampnagel
Barmbeker Straße 6a
22303 Hamburg
Germany
T +49.40.689 42 10
F +49.40.68 94 21 30
info@joi-design.com
www.joi-design.com
► 10, 30, 96

**Jan Kleihues, Kleihues + Kleihues
Gesellschaft von Architekten mbH**

Helmholtzstraße 42
10587 Berlin
Germany
T +49.30.39 97 79 0
F +49.30.39 97 79 77
berlin@kleihues.com
www.kleihues.com
► 214

Kengo Kuma & Architects

2-24-8 BY- CUBE 2-4F
Minamiaoyama Minato-ku
Tokyo 107- 0062
Japan
T +81.3.34 01 77 21
F +81.3.34 01 77 78
kuma@ba2.so-net.ne.jp
www.kkaa.co.jp
► 42

Åke Larsson

Marknadsvägen 63
981 Jukkasjärvi
Sweden
T +46.980.668 00
F +46.980.668 90
info@icehotel.com
www.icehotel.com
► 58

**Xavier Leibar – Jean-Marie
Seigneurin**

Haristéguy, 2 chemin de la Marouette
64 100 Bayonne
France
T +33.5.59 47 32 60
F +33.5.59 47 40 52
lsarchitectes@leibarseigneurin.com
www.leibarseigneurin.com
► 26

Petros Makridis + Associates

49, Antheon St.
54646 Thessaloniki
Greece
T +30.2310.42 72 22
F +30.2310.42 91 91
info@pmakridis.com
www.pmakridis.com
► 100, 176

Simone Micheli Architectural Hero

T +39.055.69 12 16
F +39.055.650 44 98
simone@simonemicheli.com
www.simonemicheli.com
Via Aretina 197 / R
50136 Firenze
Italy
► 122

Ministry of Design

16B Trengganu Street
Singapore 058470
Singapore
T +65.62 22 57 80
F +65.62 22 57 81
studio@modonline.com
www.modonline.com
► 38

Jordan Mozer and Associates Limited

320 West Ohio Street, Floor Seven
Chicago, ILL 60610
USA
T +1.312.397 11 33
F +1.312.397 12 33
jordan@mozer.com
www.mozer.com
► 226

Claudio Nardi Architetto

Via Ippolito Pindemonte, 63
50124 Firenze
Italy
T +39.055.22 21 32
F +39.055.233 59 04
info@claudionardi.it
www.claudionardi.it
► 52

Pascal Arquitectos

Atlaltunco 99
Col. Lomas de Tecamachalco,
CP 53 970
Mexico
T +52.55.52 94 23 71
F +52.55.52 94 85 13
pascal@pascalarquitectos.com
www.pascalarquitectos.com
► 180

Álvaro Planchuelo

C/ Santa Engracia 30, 6ºB
Madrid 28010
Spain
T +34.91.447 49 32
F +34.91.448 04 57
estudio@alvaroplanchuelo.com
www.alvaroplanchuelo.com
► 14

Germán del Sol – Architect

Camino Las Flores 11.441
Las Condes, Santiago
Chile
T +56.22.14 12 14
F +56.22.14 11 47
contacto@germandelsol.cl
www.germandelsol.cl
► 254

studio Gaia, Inc.

601 West 26th Street, Suite 415
New York, NY 10001
USA
T +1.212.680 35 00
F +1.212.680 35 35
contact@studiogaia.com
www.studiogaia.com
► 160

Matteo Thun & Partners S.r.l.

Via Appiani 9
20121 Milan
Italy
T +39.02.655 69 11
F +39.02.657 06 46
info@matteothun.com
www.matteothun.com
► 68, 210

Kim Utzon Arkitekter

Nordre Toldbod 23
1259 København K
Denmark
T +45.33 39 43 34
F +45.33 39 43 35
info@kimutzon.dk
www.kimutzon.dk
► 222

Gert Wingårdh / Wingårdh Arkitektkontor AB

Kungsgatan 10A
411 19 Gotheburg
Sweden
T +46.31.743 70 00
F +46.31.711 98 38
wingardhs@wingardhs.se
www.wingardhs.se
► 218

Hotel Index

Alhanatis, Minos 100 b., 101-103
Ano, Daici 42-47
Avcioglu, Ozlem 78, 79, 81 b., Portrait: Gokhan Avcioglu
Bekman, Ali 80 a., 81 a., m.
Bennetts, Peter 64
Bielsa, Christophe 92, 93

Picture Credits